AMERICAN
PRESIDENTS
IN "QUOTES"

INSPIRATION, WIT AND VERBAL GAFFES FROM THE LEADERS OF THE USA

"**Folks are usually about as happy** as **they make their minds up to be.**"

Abraham Lincoln, quoted by Orison Marden in *How to Get What You Want*, 1917.

Abraham Lincoln just before his Presidential inauguration in 1861.

AMERICAN PRESIDENTS
IN "QUOTES"

INSPIRATION, WIT AND VERBAL GAFFES FROM THE
LEADERS OF THE USA

AMMONITE PRESS

PRESS
ASSOCIATION
Images

First Published 2013 by
Ammonite Press
an imprint of AE Publications Ltd,
166 High Street, Lewes, East Sussex, BN7 1XU, United Kingdom

Images © Press Association, 2013,
except pages 35 and 39 © Library of Congress, 2013
Copyright © in the Work AE Publications Ltd, 2013

ISBN 978-1-78145-043-7

British Cataloguing in Publication Data. A catalogue record of this book is available
from the British Library.

Series Editor: Richard Wiles
Designer: Robin Shields
Picture research: Press Associaton

Colour reproduction by GMC Reprographics
Printed in China

"Forgive your enemies, but **never forget** their names."

John F. Kennedy, quoted by Ed Koch in *Mayor*, 1984.

President John F. Kennedy during a news conference in November, 1963

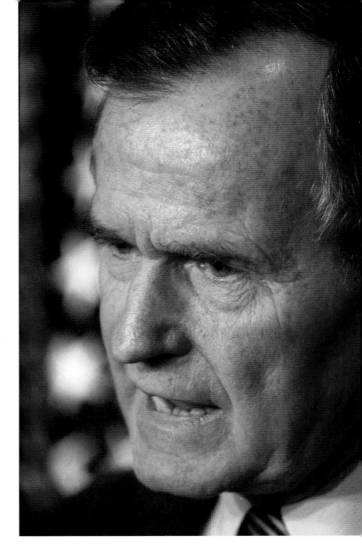

"It's no exaggeration to say that the undecideds could go **one way or another**."

George H.W. Bush, 1988.

President George H.W. Bush briefs the press in Washington, DC.

Introduction

The President of the United States of America is the most powerful person in the world, the leader of the planet's foremost economic and military power with unparalleled global reach. The nation's GDP is close to a quarter of the world's total and its military budget is almost as great as the rest of the world's military expenditure put together. So when an American President speaks, everyone listens, even when he may not have anything of great interest to say or when, occasionally, what he does say doesn't make sense.

Since George Washington became the first President of the United States in 1789, 42 men have occupied that powerful position, some more memorably than others. Many of them have been great orators, whose words have given hope and inspiration to the American people, and even the world during difficult times (Franklin D. Roosevelt: "We… would rather die on our feet than live on our knees."; John F. Kennedy: "…as a free man, I take pride in the words, '*Ich bin ein Berliner!*'"); some have had very little of note to say and some have sought to deceive (Richard Nixon: "There will be no whitewash in the White House."; Bill Clinton: "I did not have sexual relations with that woman, Monica Lewinsky."); while at times others have displayed fortitude (Theodore Roosevelt, after an assassination attempt: "I am a little sore. Anybody has a right to be a little sore with a bullet in him."; Ronald Reagan, to his wife after being shot: "Honey, I forgot to duck."), and humour, occasionally unintentionally (James A. Garfield: "Man cannot live by bread alone; he must have peanut butter."; Gerald Ford: "I watch a lot of baseball on the radio.").

Of course, there have also been a few who have managed to put their feet firmly in their mouths (Ronald Reagan: "I am pleased to tell you today that I've signed legislation that will outlaw Russia forever. We begin bombing in five minutes."; George W. Bush: "They misunderestimated me.").

Illustrated with over 120 photographs from the vast archives of the Press Association, Associated Press and Library of Congress, this book is a celebration of the political rhetoric, wisdom, humour and gaffes that have been spoken and written by those 43 Presidents of the United States over the past 224 years.

GEORGE WASHINGTON

1st President of the United States
In office: 13th July, 1789–4th March, 1797

"Liberty, when it begins to take root, is a plant of rapid growth."

"Happiness and moral duty are inseparably connected."

Letter to the bishops and clergy of the Protestant Episcopal Church, 19th August, 1789.

A Presidential dollar coin, issued by the US Mint, depicting George Washington.

"It is better to offer **no excuse** than a bad one."

Letter to his niece, Harriet Washington, 30th October, 1791.

Above: President George Washington (L) and members of his cabinet: (L–R) General Henry Knox, Secretary of War; Alexander Hamilton, Secretary of the Treasury; Thomas Jefferson, Secretary of State; and Edmund Randolph, Attorney General.

Right: This painting of Washington was rescued from the Capitol building in Washington, DC, in 1814 after it had been set on fire by the British during the War of 1812 (via Library of Congress).

JOHN ADAMS

2nd President of the United States
In office: 4th March, 1797–4th March, 1801

"Old minds are like old horses; you must exercise them if you wish to keep them in working order."

Quoted by Josiah Quincy III in *Looking Toward Sunset: from Sources Old and New, Original and Selected* by Lydia Maria Francis Child, 1865.

A contemporary steel engraving depicting John Adams.

THOMAS JEFFERSON

3rd President of the United States
In office: 4th March, 1801–4th March, 1809

"The tree of liberty must be refreshed from time to time with the blood of **patriots** and **tyrants**."

Letter to William Stephens Smith,
13th November, 1787.

Climbers use pressure washers to clean the face of Thomas Jefferson
at Mount Rushmore National Memorial in South Dakota.
26th July, 2005

"We never repent of having eaten too little."

Decalogue of Canons for Observation in Practical Life,
letter to the infant Thomas Jefferson Smith, 21st February, 1825.

Charles Julien Fevret de Saint Memin's engraving of President Thomas Jefferson for a medallion, 1804.

"We hold these truths to be self-evident, that all men are created equal; that they are endowed by their Creator with inherent and inalienable Rights; that among these are **Life, Liberty and the pursuit of Happiness.**"

Declaration of Independence, 1776.

The scene on 4th July, 1776, when the Declaration of Independence was approved by the Continental Congress in Philadelphia, Pennsylvania.

"The man who never looks into a newspaper is **better informed** than he who reads them."

Letter to John Norvell,
11th June, 1807.

A portrait of Thomas Jefferson by Rembrandt Peale, 1800.

JAMES MADISON

4th President of the United States
In office: 4th March, 1809–4th March, 1817

"The truth is that all men having power ought to be mistrusted."

Quoted by George Seldes in *The Great Quotations*, 1960.

A portrait of James Madison (via Library of Congress).

JAMES MONROE

5th President of the United States
In office: 4th March, 1817–4th March, 1825

"Preparation for war is a constant stimulus to suspicion and ill will."

A portrait of President James Monroe.

Sculptor Attilio Piccirilli working on the statue of President James Monroe at Ash Lawn-Highland, Monroe's former home near Charlottesville, Virginia. April, 1932

A 1920s 10-cent stamp bearing the portrait of President James Monroe.
5th September, 2006

"A little **flattery** will support a man through great fatigue."

JOHN Q. ADAMS

6th President of the United States
In office: 4th March, 1825–4th March, 1829

"America does not go abroad in search of monsters to destroy."

Speech, 4th July, 1821

An engraving of John Quincy Adams.

ANDREW JACKSON

7th President of the United States
In office: 4th March, 1829–4th March, 1837

"It is a **damn poor mind** indeed which can't think of at least two ways to spell any word."

Thought to be a retort to John Quincy Adams' statement that Jackson was "a barbarian who could not write a sentence of grammar and could hardly spell his own name."

Andrew Jackson in later life, c.1844.

MARTIN VAN BUREN

8th President of the United States
In office: 4th March, 1837–4th March, 1841

"As to the Presidency, the two happiest days of my life were those of my **entrance upon** the office and **my surrender of it**."

Martin Van Buren, c.1860.

WILLIAM H. HARRISON

9th President of the United States
In office: 4th March, 1841–4th April, 1841

"To Englishmen, life is a topic, not an activity."

An engraving by James Henry Beard depicting William Henry Harrison, c.1841 (Library of Congress).

WILLIAM HENRY HARRISON,
9th President of the United States,
Born Febr 9th 1773, died April 4th 1841.

By T. Campbell from the Original by J.R. Beard.   Printed by Klauprech & Menzel, Cincinnati.

JOHN TYLER

10th President of the United States
In office: 4th April, 1841–4th March, 1845

"Popularity, I have always thought, may aptly be compared to a **coquette** – the more you **woo her**, the more apt is she to **elude your embrace**."

Speech to US House of Representatives, 1816.

A contemporary engraving depicting John Tyler.

JAMES K. POLK

11th President of the United States
In office: 4th March, 1845–4th March, 1849

"With me it is exceptionally true that the Presidency is **no** bed of roses."

A daguerreotype depicting President James K. Polk, c.1860 (Library of Congress).

ZACHARY TAYLOR

12th President of the United States
In office: 4th March, 1849–9th July, 1850

"I have always done my duty. I am **ready to die.** My only regret is for the friends I leave behind me."

A portrait of Zachary Taylor, by Joseph H. Bush.

MILLARD FILLMORE

13th President of the United States
In office: 9th July, 1850–4th March, 1853

"An **honourable defeat** is better than a **dishonourable victory.**"

Millard Fillmore, c.1850.

FRANKLIN PIERCE

14th President of the United States
In office: 4th March, 1853–4th March, 1857

"Frequently the more trifling the subject, the more **animated** and **protracted** the discussion."

Franklin Pierce, c.1840.

JAMES BUCHANAN

15th President of the United States
In office: 4th March, 1857–4th March, 1861

"The ballot box is the surest **arbiter** of disputes among free men."

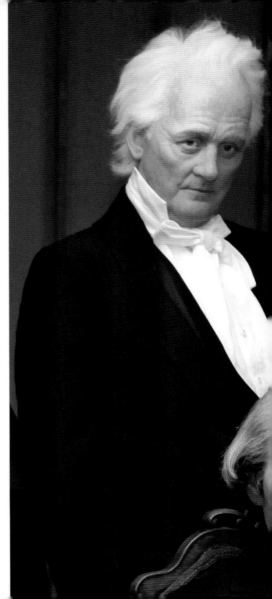

Wax figures of American Presidents at Madame Tussauds: (L–R) James Buchanan, Grover Cleveland, Chester Alan Arthur, and (foreground) Andrew Johnson.

ABRAHAM LINCOLN

16th President of the United States
In office: 4th March, 1861–15th April, 1865

"The Lord prefers common-looking people. That is why he made so many of them."

Conversation with his private secretary, John Hay, 23rd December, 1863.

One of the last photographs taken of President Abraham Lincoln before he was shot dead by John Wilkes Booth on 14th April, 1865, at Ford's Theatre, Washington, DC.
5th February, 1865

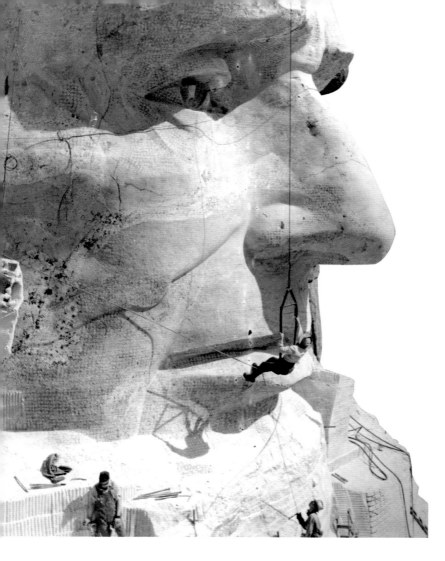

"Whatever you are, be a good one."

Sculptor Lincoln Borglum at work on the face of President Abraham Lincoln on the Mount Rushmore Memorial, near Keystone, South Dakota, c.1941.

"When I hear a man preach, I like to see him act as if he were fighting bees."

President Abraham Lincoln at the dedication of the Soldiers' National Cemetery at Gettysburg, Pennsylvania, during the Civil War, November, 1863.

"I have always found that **mercy** bears richer fruits than strict justice."

Quoted in *Lincoln Memorial*, 1882.

The 19-feet-high (5.8-metre) statue of a seated Abraham Lincoln at the Lincoln Memorial in Washington, DC.

ANDREW JOHNSON

17th President of the United States
In office: 15th April, 1865–4th March, 1869

"If I am to be shot at, I want **no man** to be in the way of the bullet."

While military governor of Tennessee following threats on his life.

Andrew Johnson, c.1865.

ULYSSES S. GRANT

18th President of the United States
In office: 4th March, 1869–4th March, 1877

"I never wanted to get out of a place as much as I did to get out of the Presidency."

Quoted by John Russell Young in *Around the World with General Grant*, vol. 2, 1879.

Hero of the Civil War, Ulysses S. Grant, 1868.

"I know only two tunes: one of them is 'Yankee Doodle', and the other one isn't."

Quoted by John Tasker Howard in *Our Contemporary Composers: American Music in the Twentieth Century*, 1941.

General Ulysses S. Grant during the Battle of Cold Harbor in Virginia, June, 1864.

RUTHERFORD B. HAYES

19th President of the United States
In office: 4th March, 1877–4th March, 1881

"Abolish **plutocracy** if you would abolish poverty. ...The more millionaires, the more paupers."

Diary entry, 16th February, 1890.

"Fighting battles is like courting girls: those who make the most pretensions and are boldest usually **win**."

Quoted by William A. DeGregorio in *The Complete Book of U.S. Presidents*, 1991.

A portrait of Rutherford B. Hayes, 1877.

JAMES A. GARFIELD

20th President of the United States
In office: 4th March, 1881–19th
September, 1881

"Man cannot live by bread alone; he must have peanut butter."

A portrait of James A. Garfield, c.1881.

"A pound of pluck is worth a ton of luck."

Speech at Spencerian Business College, Washington, DC, 29th July, 1869.

The shooting of President James A. Garfield by Charles Guiteau on 2nd July, 1881; he died 17 days later.

CHESTER A. ARTHUR

21st President of the United States
In office: 19th September, 1881–4th
March, 1885

A portrait of Chester A. Arthur, c.1882.

"I may be President of the United States, but my private life is nobody's **damn** business."

To a temperance campaigner.

GROVER CLEVELAND

22nd and 24th President of the United States
In office: 4th March, 1885–4th March, 1889;
4th March, 1893–4th March, 1897

"A man is known by the company he **keeps**, and also by the company from which he is **kept out**."

A portrait of Grover Cleveland, 1892.

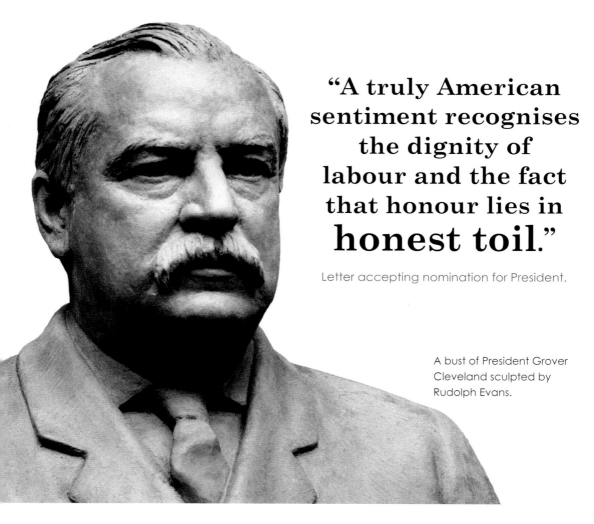

"A truly American sentiment recognises the dignity of labour and the fact that honour lies in **honest toil.**"

Letter accepting nomination for President.

A bust of President Grover Cleveland sculpted by Rudolph Evans.

The Statue of Liberty, a gift from France to the United States, stands in New York City harbour and was dedicated on 28th October, 1886, by President Cleveland.

"Communism is a hateful thing, and a menace to peace and organised government."

Fourth Annual Message, 3rd December, 1888.

BENJAMIN HARRISON

23rd President of the United States
In office: 4th March, 1889–4th March, 1893

"We Americans have no commission from God to police the world."

Statement, 1888.

A portrait of Benjamin Harrison, c.1896.

WILLIAM MCKINLEY

25th President of the United States
In office: 4th March, 1897–14th
September, 1901

"That's all a man can hope for during his lifetime – to set an example – and when he is dead, to be an **inspiration** for history."

President William McKinley (L) contemplates the 1900 Presidential campaign with his running mate Theodore Roosevelt.

THEODORE ROOSEVELT

26th President of the United States
In office: 14th September, 1901–4th
March, 1909

"Keep your eyes on the stars, but remember to keep your feet on the ground."

Speech, Groton, Massachusetts, 24th May, 1904.

Theodore Roosevelt gives a rousing speech in 1912.

"A vote is like a rifle; its usefulness depends upon the **character** of the user."

Quoted in *Theodore Roosevelt – An Autobiography*, 1913.

A young Theodore Roosevelt poses as a 'frontiersman' for a studio photo, 1885.

"The worst of all fears is the
fear of living."

Quoted in Theodore Roosevelt – An Autobiography, 1913.

Colonel Theodore Roosevelt (C) with troops of the First US Volunteer Cavalry
Regiment during the Cuban War of Independence, 1898.

"Speak softly and carry a big stick; you will go far."

Letter to Henry L. Sprague, 26th January, 1900.

Theodore Roosevelt in his office at the White House in Washington, DC, December, 1908.

"I am all right – I am a little sore. Anybody has a right to be sore with a **bullet** in him."

Speech, Milwaukee, Wisconsin, following an attempt on his life by John Schrank. Roosevelt's notes for his speech absorbed the force of the bullet, preventing it from reaching his heart, 14th October, 1912.

Theodore Roosevelt's broad smile was a trademark of the 1912 Presidential campaign.

WILLIAM H. TAFT

27th President of the United States
In office: 4th March, 1909–4th March, 1913

"I am President now and tired of being kicked around."

William Howard Taft shortly after his resignation as Chief Justice in 1930.

"Don't write so that you can be understood, write so that you **can't be misunderstood**."

William Howard Taft, 1912.

WOODROW WILSON

28th President of the United States
In office: 4th March, 1913–4th March, 1921

"If a dog will not come to you after he has looked you in the face, you ought to go home and examine your conscience."

Woodrow Wilson on his 65th birthday, 29th December, 1921.

"I not only use all the brains that I have, but all that I can **borrow**."

Speech to National Press Club, Washington, DC, 20th March, 1914.

President Woodrow Wilson in his office, c.1917.

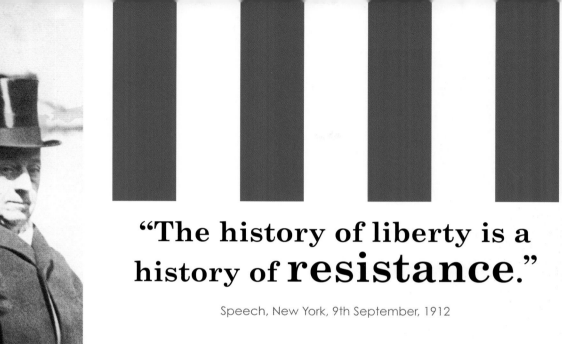

"The history of liberty is a history of **resistance**."

Speech, New York, 9th September, 1912

President Woodrow Wilson (L) rides with his successor, Warren G. Harding (second L), to the latter's inauguration, 4th March, 1921.

WARREN G. HARDING

29th President of the United States
In office: 4th March, 1921–2nd August, 1923

"I am not fit for this office and should **never** have been here."

Quoted by Nicholas Murray Butler in *Across the Busy Years*, vol. 1, 1939.

Warren G. Harding, c.1921.

"Only solitary men know the full joys of friendship. Others have their family; but to a solitary and an exile, his **friends** are everything."

President Warren G. Harding tries out a new tractor.

CALVIN COOLIDGE

30th President of the United States
In office: 2nd August, 1923–4th March, 1929

"No man ever listened himself out of a job."

President Calvin Coolidge (second L) with actor John Drew (L) and singer Al Jolson (second R) at the White House, October, 1924.

"When more and more people are thrown out of work, unemployment results."

Quoted in the *Heretic's Handbook of Quotations*, 1992.

"If you don't say anything, you won't be called on to repeat it."

President Coolidge wears a feathered headdress after being adopted as Chief Leading Eagle of the Sioux tribe, the first white man to be so honoured. 1927

President Calvin Coolidge and his wife Grace, 1923.

"There is no force so democratic as the force of an ideal."

Speech, 27th November, 1920.

Helen Keller, author and political activist, with President Calvin Coolidge at the White House, 1926.

"There is no **dignity** quite so impressive, and no independence quite so important, as living within your means."

Quoted in the *Autobiography of Calvin Coolidge*, 1929.

HERBERT HOOVER

31st President of the United States
In office: 4th March, 1929–4th March, 1933

"I'm the **only** person of distinction who has ever had a depression named for him."

Quoted by Richard Norton Smith in *An Uncommon Man*, 1984.

Inventor and businessman Thomas Edison (R) and President-elect
Herbert Hoover on Edison's 82nd birthday, 12th February, 1929.

"I outlived the bastards."

Referring to how he had dealt with people who blamed him for the Great Depression, quoted by William O. Douglas in *The Court Years 1939–75*, 1980.

Presidential hopeful Herbert Hoover with his pet dog, King Tut, 1928 (via Library of Congress).

"All men are equal before fish."

Former President Herbert Hoover goes fishing, 1939.

FRANKLIN D. ROOSEVELT

32nd President of the United States
In office: 4th March, 1933–12th April, 1945

"He's a son-of-a-bitch, but he's OUR son-of-a-bitch."

Referring to Nicaraguan President Anastasio Somoza Garcia. c.1940s.

Democratic Presidential nominee Franklin D. Roosevelt (R) and John Nance Garner, Vice Presidential nominee, stand on the rear of Roosevelt's private train at Topeka, Kansas, 1932.

"We... would rather **die on our feet** than live on our knees."

Speech, June, 1941.

A statue of Franklin D. Roosevelt in Washington, DC.

"**When you get to the end of your rope,**
tie a knot and **hang on.**"

Quoted in the *Kansas City Star*, 5th June, 1977.

"War is a contagion."

Speech, Chicago, Illinois,
5th October, 1937.

British Prime Minister Winston Churchill (L) and President Franklin D. Roosevelt at the White House in Washington, DC, 24th May, 1943.

"If the fires of freedom and civil liberties burn low in other lands, they must be made **brighter** in our own."

Speech to the National Education Association, 30th June, 1938.

President Franklin D. Roosevelt addresses a joint session of the Senate and House in Washington, DC, 16th May, 1940.

"I think we consider too much the good luck of the early bird and not enough the bad luck of the early worm."

Quoted by Connie Robertson in *The Wordsworth Dictionary of Quotations*, 1998.

Franklin D. Roosevelt hams it up for the press, March, 1943.

"Be sincere, be brief, **be seated.**"

Advice to his son James on public speaking, quoted by Paul L. Soper in *Basic Public Speaking*, 1963.

HARRY S. TRUMAN

33rd President of the United States
In office: 12th April, 1945–20th
January, 1953

President Harry S. Truman delivers his acceptance speech following his nomination as Democratic Presidential candidate, 14th July, 1948.

"I have found the best way to give advice to your children is to find out what they want and then advise them to **do it.**"

During televised interview with Edward R. Murrow, 27th May, 1955.

Harry S. Truman is given a haircut by Frank Spina, who had served with him during the First World War, August, 1944.

"It's a recession when your neighbour loses his job; it's a depression when you lose yours."

Quoted in *The Observer*, 13th April, 1958.

"Richard Nixon is a **no-good, lying bastard.** He can lie out of both sides of his mouth at the same time, and if he ever caught himself telling the truth, he'd lie just to keep his hand in."

President Harry S. Truman (L) is greeted by US General Dwight D. Eisenhower in Antwerp, Belgium, at the close of the Second World War, 20th July, 1945.

"My choice early in life was either to be a piano-player in a whorehouse or a politician. And to tell the truth there's hardly any difference."

Quoted in *Esquire* magazine, vol. 76, 1971.

President Harry S. Truman at his desk, September, 1948.

DWIGHT D. EISENHOWER

34th President of the United States
In office: 20th January, 1953–20th
January, 1961

"In preparing for battle, I have always found that plans are useless, but planning is **indispensable**."

Quoted by Richard Nixon in
Six Crises, 1962.

Vice President Richard Nixon (R) meets with President Dwight D. Eisenhower at the White House in Washington, DC. Behind stands Milton Eisenhower, the President's brother, 5th August, 1959.

President Dwight D. Eisenhower awards the National Security Medal to FBI chief J. Edgar Hoover in Washington, 27th May, 1955.

"An intellectual is a man who takes **more words** than necessary to tell more than he knows."

"Oh, that lovely title: **ex-President**."

President Dwight D. Eisenhower and his wife Mamie wave to spectators during his inauguration parade, 20th January, 1953.

President Dwight D. Eisenhower makes a radio and television broadcast, 1959.

"What counts is not necessarily the size of the dog in the fight – it's the size of the **fight in the dog.**"

Speech to the Republican National Committee, 31st January, 1958.

"The hand of the aggressor is stayed by strength – and **strength alone**."

Speech to English Speaking Union, 3rd July, 1951.

Soviet leader Nikita Khrushchev (L) with President Dwight D. Eisenhower in Washington, DC, 1959.

JOHN F. KENNEDY

35th President of the United States
In office: 20th January, 1961–22nd
November, 1963

"And so, my fellow Americans: ask not what your country can do for you – ask what **you** can do for your country."

Inaugural Address, Washington, DC,
20th January, 1961.

President John F. Kennedy makes
a speech, 1962.

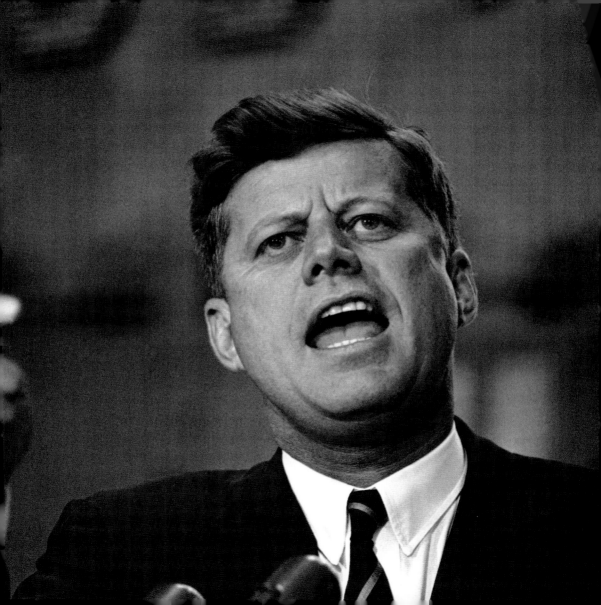

"Let every nation know, whether it wishes us well or ill, that we shall **pay any price**, bear any burden, meet any hardship, support any friend, oppose any foe to assure the survival and the **success of liberty**."

Inaugural Address, Washington, DC, 20th January, 1961.

John F. Kennedy, makes a point during the Presidential campaign of 1960.

"The only valid **test of leadership** is the ability to lead, and lead vigorously."

Presidential Nomination Acceptance Speech, Democratic National Convention, Los Angeles, California, 15th July, 1960.

John F. Kennedy reads newspaper accounts of his West Virginia election victory. He had defeated Senator Hubert Humphrey in the previous day's Presidential primary, 11th May, 1960.

"I wonder how it is with you, Harold? If I don't have a **woman** for three days, I get terrible headaches."

In conversation with British Prime Minister Harold Macmillan, quoted by Richard Reeves in *President Kennedy: Profile of Power*, 1994.

British Prime Minister Harold Macmillan (R) with President John F. Kennedy, who was on a brief visit for informal talks, June, 1963.

"**America has tossed its cap over the wall of space**, and we have no choice but to follow it."

Speech, Aerospace Medical Center, San Antonio, Texas, November, 1963.

John F. Kennedy and his wife Jacqueline at New York's Idlewild Airport in New York City, July, 1960.

"All free men, wherever they may live, are citizens of Berlin. And therefore, as a free man, I take pride in the words, 'Ich bin ein Berliner!' (I am a Berliner)."

Speech concerning the reunification of Germany, Rathaus Schöneberg, West Berlin, Germany, 26th June, 1963.

President John F. Kennedy makes the famous speech at Schöneberg town hall in West Berlin, 26th June, 1963.

LYNDON B. JOHNSON

36th President of the United States
In office: 22nd November, 1963–20th
January, 1969

"Being president is like being a **jackass** in a hailstorm. There's nothing to do but to stand there and take it."

President Lyndon B. Johnson appears exasperated by this telephone conversation, 1964.

"Jerry Ford is so **dumb** he can't fart and chew gum at the same time."

Vice President Lyndon B. Johnson reports to President John F. Kennedy on his recent tour of Scandinavian countries, September, 1963.

"I have learned that only two things are necessary to keep one's wife happy. First, let her think she's having her own way. And second, let her have it."

Lady Bird and President Lyndon B. Johnson at their ranch near Stonewall, Texas, September, 1967.

President Johnson rounds up cattle on his ranch in Texas, November, 1964.

"You might say that Lyndon Johnson is a cross between a **Baptist preacher and a cowboy.**"

"A President's hardest task is not to do what is right, but to **know** what is right."

President Lyndon B. Johnson makes a point, 1967.

RICHARD NIXON

37th President of the United States
In office: 20th January, 1969–9th
August, 1974

"There will be no whitewash in the White House."

Televised speech concerning the Watergate affair: five men, later shown to have links to the Republican Party, had been arrested the previous year breaking into the Democratic Party's Watergate headquarters with photographic and bugging equipment, an event that would lead to Nixon's downfall only months after his re-election, 30th April, 1973.

Republican Presidential candidate Richard Nixon makes his acceptance speech at the GOP Convention in Miami Beach, Florida, 9th August, 1968.

"**People have got to know whether or not their president is a crook. Well, I'm not a crook. I earned everything I've got.**"

Televised press conference, Walt Disney World, Florida, 17th November, 1973.

President Richard Nixon signs the National Cancer Act at the White House in Washington, DC, 23rd December, 1971.

"I'm **not for women**, frankly, in any job. I don't want any of them around. Thank God we don't have any in the Cabinet."

Quoted by John Dean in *The Rehnquist Choice*, 2001.

Soviet leader Leonid Brezhnev (L) spills his champagne as he and President Richard Nixon prepare to drink a toast at the State Department in Washington, DC, 19th June, 1973.

"I let the American people down."

President Richard Nixon makes a point during a news conference, June, 1972.

GERALD FORD

38th President of the United States
In office: 9th August, 1974–20th
January, 1977

"If Lincoln were alive today, he'd be turning over in his grave."

President Gerald Ford makes a point during a National Security Council meeting in Washington, DC, May, 1975.

"The **three-martini lunch** is the epitome of American efficiency. Where else can you get an earful, a bellyful and a snootful at the same time?"

Speech to the National Restaurant Association, Chicago, Illinois, 28th May, 1978.

California Governor Ronald Reagan (R) and Vice President Gerald Ford share a joke during a lunch, April, 1974.

"I **watch** a lot of baseball on the radio."

President Gerald Ford and Queen Elizabeth II dance during the state dinner at the
White House in Washington, DC, 7th July, 1976.

JIMMY CARTER

39th President of the United States
In office: 20th January, 1977–20th
January, 1981

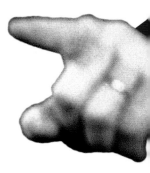

"I can't **deny** I'm a better ex-President than I was a President."

Remark to reporters in Washington, 2005.

President Jimmy Carter fields a question during a news conference, October, 1978.

"America did not invent human rights. In a very real sense, human rights **invented America**."

Farewell Address, 14th January, 1981.

Left: Hollywood actor Iron Eyes Cody presents President Jimmy Carter with a Native American headdress at the White House in Washington, DC, 21st April, 1978.

"Aggression unopposed becomes a contagious disease."

Quoted by A.Z. Hilali in *US-Pakistan Relationship: Soviet Invasion Of Afghanistan*, 2005.

President Jimmy Carter prepares to sign his economic, tax and budget messages, 20th January, 1978.

RONALD REAGAN

40th President of the United States
In office: 20th January, 1981–20th
January, 1989

"The nine most terrifying words in the English language are, 'I'm from the government and I'm here to help.'"

Speech, 12th August, 1986.

President Ronald Reagan jokes with photographers in the Oval Office of the White House in Washington, DC, October, 1983.

"Honey, I forgot to **duck**."

To his wife Nancy, after surviving an assassination attempt, 30th March, 1981.

President Ronald Reagan is shot by John Hinckley outside a Washington hotel, 30th March, 1981.

President Ronald Reagan at a news conference at the White House, Washington, DC, June, 1984.

"My fellow Americans, I am pleased to tell you today that I've signed legislation that will outlaw Russia forever. We begin **bombing** in five minutes."

Joke during a microphone check, 11th August, 1984.

President Ronald Reagan stops off for a Big Mac, October, 1984.

"I never drink coffee at lunch. I find it keeps me **awake** for the afternoon."

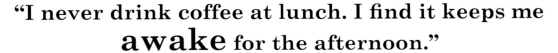

President Ronald Reagan (L) welcomes Soviet leader Mikhail Gorbachev to a summit in Reykjavik, Iceland, 10th October, 1986.

"Mr Gorbachev, **tear** down this wall!"

Speech, referring to the wall separating East Berlin from West Berlin, Brandenburg Gate, Berlin, Germany, 12th June, 1987.

GEORGE H.W. BUSH

41st President of the United States
In office: 20th January, 1989–20th
January, 1993

"Fluency in English is something that I'm often **not** accused of."

Right: Soviet leader Mikhail Gorbachev (L) with President George H.W. Bush during a news conference at the White House, Washington, DC, 3rd June, 1990.

"But let me tell you, this gender thing is history. You're looking at a guy who sat down with Margaret Thatcher across the table and talked about **serious** issues."

Vice President George H.W. Bush enjoys a joke with Britain's Prime Minister Margaret Thatcher, 3rd July, 1985.

"I have opinions of my own, **strong opinions**, but I don't always agree with them."

Former President George H.W. Bush checks his bell before ringing it to encourage passers-by in Houston, Texas, to donate to the Salvation Army's Christmas charity appeal, December, 2006.

"I like a **colourful** sock. I'm a sock man."

Former President George H.W. Bush and his wife Barbara arrive at the White House in Washington, DC, May, 2012.

BILL CLINTON

42nd President of the United States
In office: 20th January, 1993–20th
January, 2001

"Being President is like being the groundskeeper in a cemetery: you've got a lot of people under you and none of them are listening."

Bill Clinton plays the saxophone during the Arsenio Hall TV show, 3rd June, 1992.

"I **did not** have sexual relations with that woman, Monica Lewinsky."

Televised address, 26th January, 1998. The denial led to an impeachment charge of perjury.

President Bill Clinton and White House intern Monica Lewinsky in November, 1995.
She claimed that she had had nine sexual encounters with him in the Oval Office.

"Indeed, I **did** have a relationship with Miss Lewinsky that was not appropriate."

Televised address, 17th August, 1998.

Hillary Clinton watches President Bill Clinton as he thanks the Democratic members of the House of Representatives who voted against his impeachment, 19th December, 1998.

Wax sculptures of Bill Clinton and Socks, the Presidential cat, on display at the Grévin Museum in Paris, France.

"When I took office, only high-energy physicists had ever heard of what is called the worldwide web... Now even my cat has its own page."

Announcement of the Next Generation Internet Initiative, 1996

"The future is **not** an inheritance, it is an opportunity and an obligation."

President Bill Clinton and Vice President Al Gore during a ceremony in the Rose Garden of the White House in Washington, DC, October, 1998.

GEORGE W. BUSH

43rd President of the United States
In office: 20th January, 2001–20th
January, 2009

"When I take action, I'm not going to fire a $2 million missile at a $10 empty tent and hit a camel in the butt. It's going to be decisive."

Remark to a group of Senators, quoted in *Newsweek*, 24th September, 2001.

President George W. Bush addresses American service personnel in South Korea, November, 2005.

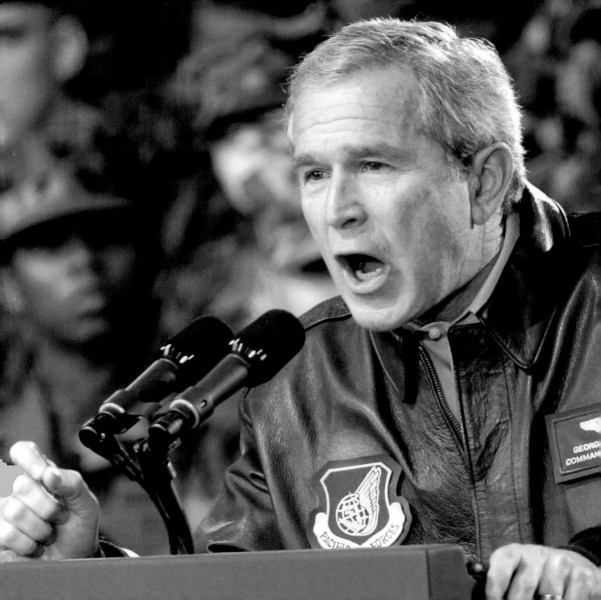

"Yo Blair, how are you doin'?"

To British Prime Minister Tony Blair, G8 Summit, unaware that his microphone was switched on, 17th July, 2006.

British Prime Minister Tony Blair and President George W. Bush outside 10 Downing Street, London, 20th November, 2003.

President George W. Bush and his wife Laura at the unveiling of their official portraits in Washington, DC, 19th December, 2008.

"I suspected there would be a good-size crowd once the word got out about my hanging."

Remark during the unveiling of his national portrait, 19th December, 2008.

"I know the human being and fish can **co-exist** peacefully."

Explaining his energy policies, Michigan, September, 2000.

President George W. Bush with a striped bass that he had caught off the coast of Maine, June, 2003.

"They **misunderestimated** me."

Explaining his unexpected victories over John McCain in the 2000 Presidential Primaries, 6th November, 2000.

President George W. Bush carries his dog Barney as he walks to a helicopter at Texas State Technical College in Waco, Texas, April, 2005.

BARACK OBAMA

44th President of the United States
In office: 20th January, 2009–present

"Change will not come if we wait for some other person or some other time. We are the ones we've been waiting for. **We** are the change that we seek."

Speech, 5th February, 2008.

Barack Obama makes a Presidential campaign speech, January, 2012.

"I am reminded every day of my life,
if not by events, then by my wife,
that I am **not** a perfect man."

Speech, Mitchell, South Dakota, 1st June, 2008.

President Barack Obama at the White House Easter Egg Roll, April, 2012.

"**What Washington needs is adult supervision.**"

Fund-raising letter, October, 2006.

Left: President Barack Obama, his wife Michelle and his two daughters, Malia (L) and Sasha, show off their new pet dog at the White House in Washington, DC, April, 2009.

President Barack Obama stresses a point, September, 2009.

"Americans... still believe in an America where anything's possible – they just don't think their leaders do."

Fund-raising letter, 1st September, 2006.

Right: President Barack Obama adopts a stern expression, June, 2010.

"If you're looking for the safe choice, you shouldn't be supporting a black guy named Barack Obama to be the next leader of the **free world**."

INDEX

The Publishers gratefully acknowledge the Press Association,
Associated Press and the Library of Congress, from whose extensive
archives the photographs in this book have been selected.

PRESS
ASSOCIATION
Images

AMMONITE
PRESS